"THINKING ERRORS:

REWIRING YOUR MIND FOR PEACE AND PURPOSE"

DR.VIVEK G VASOYA MD
(HOMEOPATHIC PSYCHIATRIST)

To my beloved parents,

Rsilaben gopalbhai & Gopalbhai Arjanbhai Vasoya.
For your unwavering support, endless patience, and unconditional
love.
You've been my guiding light, my greatest teachers, and my
constant inspiration.
This book is a reflection of the values and strength you've instilled
in me.
Thank you for believing in me, always.

Contents

Preface

In a world where our thoughts shape the way we live, it is astonishing how often we allow errors in our thinking to cloud our perception of reality. These thinking errors—cognitive distortions, mental traps, or simply unhelpful patterns—affect not only our decisions but also our emotional well-being, relationships, and sense of purpose.

I began this journey of exploring thinking errors as a curious observer of the human mind. Over years of study and practice, I realized that while our thoughts have immense power to create, they also have the capacity to distort and mislead us. The good news is that we don't have to be prisoners of these errors. With awareness, understanding, and practice, we can rewire our minds to think more clearly and compassionately.

This book is not merely a theoretical exploration—it's a practical guide to untangling the common mental knots that hold us back. Whether you find yourself jumping to conclusions, dwelling on worst-case scenarios, or setting unrealistic expectations for yourself, this book will help you identify these patterns and provide actionable tools to shift your mindset toward peace and purpose.

The aim of this book is simple: to help you recognize the thoughts that limit you and to empower you to create new patterns of thinking that serve your highest good. Through relatable examples, easy-to-use exercises, and insights from psychology and neuroscience, you will discover that change is not only possible—it is within your grasp.

As you turn these pages, I encourage you to approach this journey with curiosity and compassion for yourself. Each of us is a work in progress, and every step forward—however small—is a step toward clarity and growth.

This book is dedicated to everyone who has ever struggled with their inner critic, doubted their potential, or felt stuck in a cycle of unhelpful thoughts. May this guide serve as a light to help you navigate the maze of your mind, uncovering the peace and purpose that already reside within you.

Welcome to the journey of rewiring your mind.

Warm regards,
Dr. Vivek G Vasoya MD

(Homeopathic Psychiatrist)

Acknowledgements

Writing this book has been a deeply personal and transformative journey, and it would not have been possible without the support, guidance, and inspiration of many incredible individuals.

First and foremost, I want to express my heartfelt gratitude to my family, whose unwavering love and encouragement have been the foundation of my work. To my parents, who instilled in me the values of curiosity and resilience, and to my wife, her patience and belief in me gave me the strength to bring this project to life, thank you for being my constant source of inspiration.

I am deeply thankful to my mentors and colleagues in the field of psychology and medicine, whose insights and expertise have profoundly shaped my understanding of the human mind. Their invaluable guidance has enriched this book with scientific rigor and practical relevance.

To my patients and students, thank you for trusting me to be part of your journey. Your courage in confronting challenges and your openness in sharing your experiences have taught me more than any textbook ever could. You are the reason this book exists, and I hope it serves as a helpful guide for others on their path to self-discovery and growth.

I am also indebted to the researchers and thinkers whose work has paved the way for our understanding of cognitive distortions and mental health. This book stands on the shoulders of giants, and their contributions to the field of psychology have been instrumental in shaping its content.

A special thank you to my editor and publishing team for their dedication, insight, and attention to detail. Your expertise transformed my ideas into a cohesive narrative that I am proud to share with the world.

Finally, to my readers—thank you for picking up this book and trusting it to be part of your journey. Writing this for you has been an honor, and I hope it helps you find clarity, peace, and purpose.

This book is a collective effort, and I am profoundly grateful to everyone who played a role in its creation.

With deepest appreciation,
Dr. Vivek G Vasoya MD

(Homeopathic Psychiatrist)

Prologue

The Lens We See Through

Your mind is like a lens, shaping how you see the world, yourself, and others. But what if that lens was flawed—warped by invisible smudges and cracks? These distortions in thinking don't just blur your vision; they can shape your emotions, decisions, and relationships. They can make a small setback feel like a catastrophe or turn a single comment into a sign of failure.

*These invisible distortions are called **cognitive distortions**—automatic patterns of flawed thinking that affect how we interpret and respond to life's challenges. Everyone experiences them. The overachiever who feels like a fraud, the worrier who jumps to the worst-case scenario, the partner who assumes their loved one's frustration is entirely their fault—all are victims of these traps of the mind.*

But here's the good news: these patterns can be identified, challenged, and reframed. The goal of this book is to help you do just that.

You'll learn to recognize the most common cognitive

distortions, explore why they occur, and discover practical tools to break free from their grip. Whether you're struggling with anxiety, stuck in a cycle of self-doubt, or simply seeking greater clarity in your thinking, this book offers the roadmap you need to reclaim your mental freedom.

As you journey through these pages, you'll uncover the incredible resilience of the human mind. You'll see how even the most deeply ingrained thought patterns can change with effort and awareness. And you'll understand that your thoughts, while powerful, are not facts—they are a starting point, not a destination.

Let's begin by untangling the knots in our thinking and stepping into a life of clarity, confidence, and emotional balance.

CHAPTER I

What Are Cognitive Distortions?

The Thought Traps That Shape Our Reality

Imagine this: You're walking through a park on a sunny afternoon. A friend passes by and doesn't wave back. What's your immediate reaction?

For some, it might be:

"They must be upset with me. I must have done something wrong." (Personalization)

"They didn't wave because they don't like me anymore." (Mind Reading)

"This always happens. Nobody cares about me." (Overgeneralization)

Notice how quickly these interpretations arise. The event itself—a friend not waving—is neutral. It's the meaning we attach to it that determines how we feel and respond.

This is the essence of cognitive distortions: automatic, habitual patterns of thinking that skew our perception of reality. These distortions aren't just harmless quirks; they can fuel anxiety, depression, anger, and low self-esteem. Left unchecked, they can become a self-fulfilling prophecy, reinforcing negative beliefs and keeping us trapped in a cycle of distorted thinking.

The Cost of Distorted Thinking

Cognitive distortions can feel like harmless habits, but their impact is profound.

Mental Health: *Distortions are at the core of anxiety, depression, and many other psychological challenges.*

Relationships: *Misinterpretations of others' words or actions can lead to unnecessary conflict and mistrust.*

Self-Worth: *Patterns like all-or-nothing thinking or harsh self-criticism can erode confidence and resilience.*

The real tragedy of cognitive distortions is how sneaky they are. Often, we don't even realize our thoughts are distorted. They feel true—so true that we act on them, shaping our lives in their image.

*But here's the empowering part: **cognitive distortions are not permanent. They are habits of thought, and like any habit, they can be changed.***

A Roadmap for Change

This book is your guide to untangling these distorted thought patterns. Together, we'll explore:

*The **most common cognitive distortions***

*The **psychological and neurological roots** of these distortions.*

*Proven strategies to **challenge and reframe distorted thoughts**, so you can see yourself and the world more clearly.*

Practical tools to apply this knowledge in daily life—whether in relationships, at work, or in your personal growth.

The journey won't always be easy. Challenging your own thoughts can feel uncomfortable, even unsettling. But it's also one of the most liberating things you can do for yourself.

By the end of this book, you won't just understand cognitive distortions—you'll have the tools to transform them, unlocking a clearer, calmer, and more confident mind.

Let's get started.

CHAPTER II

The Science Behind Thinking Types and Cognitive Distortions

Understanding the Anatomy, Physiology, Psychodynamics, and Types of Thinking

Introduction: The Brain and the Mind

Cognitive distortions are not random occurrences. They are deeply influenced by how the brain processes information, the shortcuts it takes, and the thinking styles we develop through experience. To fully grasp why these distortions occur, we must explore the interplay between the brain's anatomy, its physiology, psychodynamics, and the different types of thinking that shape our mental processes.

*This chapter examines the brain regions and neurotransmitters responsible for distorted thinking, the shortcuts (heuristics) that lead to errors, and the psychodynamic theories that illuminate unconscious processes. Additionally, it categorizes **thinking types**—ways in which people process and approach information—and their role in fostering cognitive distortions.*

1. Anatomy and Physiology of Thinking

Key Brain Regions Involved in Thinking and Cognitive Distortions

1.Prefrontal Cortex (PFC): The Executive Center

Function:
Responsible for higher-order thinking, decision-making, and emotional regulation, the PFC helps us analyze situations rationally and suppress impulsive, emotion-driven responses.

Relevance to Cognitive Distortions:
Underactivity in the PFC, often due to stress or fatigue, diminishes its ability to counter emotional impulses from the amygdala, making us more prone to distorted thoughts like catastrophizing and black-and-white thinking.

Research Insight:
Arnsten et al. (2013) demonstrated that chronic stress impairs PFC function, weakening our ability to regulate fear-based thoughts from the amygdala.

2.Amygdala: The Emotional Alarm System

Function:
The amygdala is crucial for detecting threats and triggering survival responses, such as fight, flight, or freeze.

Relevance to Cognitive Distortions:
Hyperactivity in the amygdala amplifies fear and emotional reasoning, exaggerating perceived threats and fueling distortions like catastrophizing.

Research Insight:
Etkin et al. (2009) found heightened amygdala activity in people with anxiety disorders, correlating with tendencies to catastrophize and personalize.

3.Hippocampus: The Memory Keeper

Function:
Processes memories and connects them to emotions, enabling us to learn from past experiences.

Relevance to Cognitive Distortions:
Traumatic or negative memories stored in the hippocampus often resurface unconsciously, reinforcing overgeneralization or labeling (e.g., "I always fail because I failed once before").

Research Insight:
Bremner et al. (2004) observed reduced hippocampal

volume in trauma survivors, which impairs their ability to contextualize past events, perpetuating cognitive distortions.

Neurotransmitters and Their Role in Thinking

1.Serotonin:

Role in Thinking: *Regulates mood, emotional stability, and cognitive flexibility. Low levels of serotonin are linked to depressive thinking patterns, such as mental filtering and hopelessness.*

Research Insight: *Harmer et al. (2007) found that increasing serotonin levels through SSRIs enhanced patients' ability to process ambiguous information positively, reducing distorted interpretations.*

2.Dopamine:

Role in Thinking: *Associated with motivation and reward processing. Low dopamine levels can lead to self-critical distortions, such as labeling oneself a "failure" after setbacks.*

Research Insight: *Pizzagalli (2014) showed that individuals with depression and reduced dopamine activity had a diminished capacity to respond to* *positive feedback, reinforcing negative thought patterns.*

3.Cortisol:

Role in Thinking: *High levels of cortisol, the stress hormone, impair the PFC and enhance amygdala activity, fostering rigid, fear-based thinking.*

Research Insight: *Lupien et al. (2009) found that prolonged cortisol exposure damages the hippocampus and weakens PFC regulation, making individuals more prone to distortions like catastrophizing.*

• • •

2. Types of Thinking and Their Impact on Cognitive Distortions

The way we approach problems and process information significantly influences the likelihood of cognitive distortions. Below are the most common **types of thinking**, *along with their potential to trigger or mitigate distortions:*

1. Concrete (Literal) Thinking

Focus:

Centered on specific, tangible details rather than abstract or generalized ideas.

It involves processing information in a straightforward, often narrow way.

Examples in Action:

Focusing on one small mistake in a presentation and concluding the entire event was a failure.

Taking instructions or comments literally, without interpreting nuance or underlying meaning.

Relation to Cognitive Distortions:

*Linked to distortions like **mental filtering** (fixating on the negative) or **personalization** (blaming oneself for isolated issues).*

2. Heuristic Thinking

Focus:

Heuristic thinking is a mental shortcut that simplifies decision-making by relying on quick judgments based on experience, intuition, or accessible information.

It prioritizes speed and efficiency over accuracy.

Examples in Action:

Assuming a plane is unsafe because you recently saw a news story about a crash (availability heuristic).

Trusting the first piece of information you hear in a negotiation (anchoring heuristic).

Relation to Cognitive Distortions:

*Linked to distortions like **catastrophizing** (exaggerating danger based on recent events) or **confirmation bias** (seeking evidence that supports a preconceived notion).*

3. Abstract Thinking

Definition:

The ability to process ideas, patterns, and relationships beyond immediate, observable facts.

Role in Distortions:

While abstract thinking can reduce black-and-white thinking, excessive abstraction can lead to overgeneralization (e.g., "One bad relationship means I'll always fail in love").

Example:

"I didn't get this promotion, so I'll never be successful in my career."

4. Analytical Thinking

Definition:

Breaking down complex problems into smaller components for detailed evaluation.

Role in Distortions:

Analytical thinkers are less prone to distortions when they critically evaluate their thoughts. However, overanalyzing can lead to catastrophizing or rumination.

Example:

"If I forget to send this email, my boss will think I'm irresponsible, and I'll get fired."

5. Intuitive Thinking

Definition:

Relying on gut feelings or instincts to make decisions.

Role in Distortions:

Intuitive thinkers may fall prey to emotional reasoning, equating feelings with facts (e.g., "I feel incompetent, so I must be incompetent").

Example:

"I feel anxious about this trip, so something bad must happen."

6. Critical Thinking

Definition:

Using logic and evidence to evaluate ideas and solve problems.

Role in Distortions:

Critical thinking helps individuals challenge distorted thoughts. Those with strong critical thinking skills are more likely to identify and correct cognitive errors.

Example:

"I made a mistake in this project, but I've succeeded in many others. This doesn't define my abilities."

7. Self-Reflective Thinking

Definition:

The ability to examine and evaluate one's own thoughts, emotions, and behaviors.

Role in Distortions:

Self-reflection can reduce personalization and should statements, promoting greater emotional regulation.

Example:

"I'm feeling guilty, but that doesn't mean I caused the problem. I can consider what's in my control."

• • •

3. Psychodynamic Perspectives on Cognitive Distortions

Freud's Influence: Defense Mechanisms and Distorted Thoughts

Freud's theories provide insight into the unconscious processes behind cognitive distortions:

Repression:

Overgeneralization may stem from repressed memories of failure or rejection.

Example: A repressed childhood embarrassment may lead to the belief, "I always embarrass myself."

Projection:

Personalization often reflects projecting internal insecurities onto external situations (e.g., "They must think poorly of me because I think poorly of myself").

• • •

3.Attachment Theory and Thinking Styles

Attachment theory, first introduced by John Bowlby and expanded by Mary Ainsworth, explains how early relationships with caregivers shape our emotional responses and thinking patterns throughout life. These early experiences form **attachment styles**—*patterns of relating to others that influence how we interpret situations, process information, and respond to emotions.*

Attachment styles, particularly **anxious** *and* **avoidant** *attachment, often underpin cognitive distortions by shaping expectations about relationships, trust, and emotional security. These styles influence how we perceive others' intentions and interpret emotional cues, frequently leading to distorted thought patterns.*

1. Anxious Attachment

Overview:

Anxious attachment develops when a caregiver is inconsistent—sometimes attentive and responsive, other times unavailable or unresponsive. This unpredictability creates a heightened sensitivity to rejection and a constant need for reassurance.

Characteristics of Anxious Attachment in Thinking:

1.Heightened Emotional Vigilance:

People with anxious attachment are hyperaware of changes in others' behavior, often interpreting them as signs of rejection or disapproval.

Example: If a friend takes longer than usual to reply to a text, the person may think, "They must be upset with me."

2.Fear of Abandonment:

A fear of being unloved or abandoned leads to cognitive distortions like **mind reading** *and* **catastrophizing.**

Example: After a minor disagreement, someone might think, "They're going to leave me because I upset them."

3.Overreliance on External Validation:

Anxiously attached individuals often base their self-worth on how others treat them, leading to distortions like **personalization** *(e.g., "If they're unhappy, it must be my fault").*

Common Cognitive Distortions in Anxious Attachment:

Mind Reading:

Assuming others are upset or thinking negatively about them without evidence.

Example: "They didn't say hi because they're angry with me."

Catastrophizing:

Exaggerating the worst possible outcome in relationships.

Example: "If they don't call back, it means they don't care about me anymore."

Psychological Impact:

Anxious attachment often creates cycles of overthinking and emotional distress, where distorted thoughts drive feelings of insecurity and neediness in relationships.

Research Insight:

A 2017 study by Mikulincer and Shaver found that individuals with anxious attachment are more likely to misinterpret neutral social cues as negative, leading to heightened emotional reactivity and reliance on cognitive distortions like mind reading.

2. Avoidant Attachment

Overview:

Avoidant attachment develops when caregivers are emotionally distant, dismissive, or unavailable. To cope with unmet emotional needs, the individual learns to suppress vulnerability and rely on self-sufficiency, avoiding closeness to protect themselves from rejection or disappointment.

Characteristics of Avoidant Attachment in Thinking:

1.Emotional Suppression:

Avoidantly attached individuals tend to minimize or dismiss their own and others' emotions, leading to **emotional reasoning** *and detachment.*

Example: "I feel distant, so I can't trust anyone."

2.Fear of Dependence:

They may interpret attempts at emotional closeness as threats to their autonomy, leading to **black-and-white thinking** *in relationships.*

Example: "If I open up to them, I'll lose control."

3.Distrust of Others:

*Avoidant individuals often assume others will not meet their emotional needs, leading to **mental filtering** (focusing on perceived flaws in others) or **overgeneralization** (e.g., "No one can be trusted").*

Common Cognitive Distortions in Avoidant Attachment:

1.Emotional Reasoning:

Equating feelings of distance or distrust with reality.

Example: "I feel disconnected from them, so this relationship isn't worth pursuing."

2.Black-and-White Thinking:

Viewing relationships as all good or all bad, often dismissing people entirely after minor conflicts.

Example: "They didn't support me in one situation, so I can't rely on them at all."

Psychological Impact:

Avoidant attachment often leads to emotional isolation and difficulty forming deep, meaningful connections. Cognitive distortions serve as self-protective mechanisms but ultimately reinforce loneliness and mistrust.

Research Insight:

Research by Fraley et al. (2011) highlights that individuals with avoidant attachment are more likely to suppress emotional experiences, resulting in reliance on distorted thinking patterns like emotional reasoning to justify their withdrawal from relationships.

• • •

4. Neuroplasticity and the Potential for Change

What Is Neuroplasticity?

Neuroplasticity is the brain's remarkable ability to adapt and reorganize itself by forming new neural connections throughout life. This adaptability is essential for learning, memory, recovery from injury, and reshaping thought patterns. Neuroplasticity challenges the outdated belief that the adult brain is static, emphasizing instead that our brains are dynamic and capable of change.

*This principle lies at the heart of therapies like **Cognitive Behavioral Therapy (CBT)** and **mindfulness practices**, which encourage individuals to challenge maladaptive thought patterns and replace them with healthier alternatives. Through repeated practice, these new thought patterns become ingrained, fostering emotional resilience and improved mental health.*

The Mechanisms of Neuroplasticity

1.Synaptic Plasticity:

Neuroplasticity occurs at the level of synapses (the connections between neurons). Strengthening or weakening these connections allows the brain to adapt to new experiences.

Example: When you replace a distorted thought with a more balanced one, the new thought strengthens specific neural pathways, while the old pattern weakens due to lack of use.

2.Hebbian Learning:

Often summarized as "neurons that fire together, wire together," Hebbian learning explains how repeated activation of certain thought patterns reinforces their neural connections. By redirecting thoughts toward healthier perspectives, you can "rewire" the brain for more balanced thinking.

3.Long-Term Potentiation (LTP):

This process strengthens synapses based on repeated activity. Positive thought patterns reinforced through CBT or mindfulness practices benefit from LTP, solidifying healthier neural pathways.

How Cognitive Restructuring Changes the Brain

Cognitive restructuring—a key component of CBT—leverages neuroplasticity to reshape thought patterns by challenging and replacing cognitive distortions. Here's how it works:

1. Creating New Neural Pathways

*When you identify and replace distorted thoughts with balanced, rational alternatives, you create new neural connections in the **prefrontal cortex (PFC)**. Repeatedly engaging in this practice strengthens these new pathways, making them the brain's default response over time.*

Example in Action:

Distorted Thought:

"I'll never succeed because I made a mistake."

Challenged Thought:

"One mistake doesn't define my abilities. I've succeeded many times before."

Result:

Replacing the negative thought weakens the neural connections tied to self-doubt and strengthens pathways associated with self-compassion and confidence.

Research Insight:

A study by Siegle et al. (2007) found that individuals undergoing CBT showed increased PFC activity after practicing cognitive restructuring. This change was linked to improved emotional regulation and reduced depressive symptoms.

2. Reducing Amygdala Hyperactivity

*The **amygdala**, the brain's emotional alarm system, is often overactive in individuals prone to fear-based distortions like catastrophizing or emotional reasoning. Repeated exposure to distorted thoughts activates the amygdala, reinforcing the brain's tendency to overreact to perceived threats.*

Cognitive restructuring helps reduce this hyperactivity by teaching the brain to evaluate situations more rationally. Over time, the amygdala's response becomes less intense, decreasing the emotional intensity of fear-based thoughts.

Example in Action:

Distorted Thought:

"If I speak up in this meeting, I'll embarrass myself and lose my job."

Challenged Thought:

"I've shared ideas before, and it went well. One comment won't ruin my career."

Result:

This reframing helps the amygdala "learn" that the situation is not a genuine threat, reducing its exaggerated response in future scenarios.

Research Insight:

Goldin et al. (2016) showed that mindfulness-based cognitive therapy (MBCT) effectively reduced amygdala reactivity in individuals with social anxiety disorder. This reduction correlated with fewer instances of catastrophizing and emotional reasoning.

3. Enhancing the Prefrontal Cortex (PFC)

The PFC is crucial for regulating emotions, making decisions, and overriding automatic responses from the amygdala. Practices like mindfulness and CBT directly enhance the PFC's function, increasing its capacity to:

Assess situations logically.

Evaluate evidence for and against a thought.

Suppress impulsive, emotion-driven reactions.

Example in Action:

Distorted Thought:

"I feel like everyone is judging me, so it must be true."

PFC Involvement:

The PFC evaluates this thought by analyzing evidence (e.g., "Nobody said anything negative about me today").

Result:

The PFC overrides the emotional response driven by the amygdala, leading to a more balanced interpretation.

Research Insight:

A 2013 study by Davidson and McEwen found that mindfulness meditation strengthened PFC activity, improving emotional regulation and reducing reliance on distorted thinking patterns.

Techniques That Leverage Neuroplasticity

1.Cognitive Behavioral Therapy (CBT):

CBT teaches individuals to identify and replace cognitive distortions, fostering the creation of healthier neural pathways.

Evidence:

Hofmann et al. (2012) conducted a meta-analysis showing that CBT reduces symptoms of anxiety and depression by targeting distorted thinking, with measurable changes in brain activity.

2.Mindfulness Practices:

Mindfulness strengthens the PFC and reduces amygdala hyperactivity, making the brain more resilient to stress and distortions.

Evidence:

A 2016 study by Hölzel et al. found that 8 weeks of mindfulness-based stress reduction increased PFC gray matter density and reduced stress-induced activation of the amygdala.

3.Graded Exposure Therapy:

Gradual exposure to feared situations helps retrain the brain to see them as less threatening, reducing amygdala reactivity.

4.Journaling and Thought Records:

Writing down and restructuring distorted thoughts provides repeated opportunities for cognitive reframing, reinforcing healthier neural pathways.

Neuroplasticity: A Hopeful Outlook

The brain's neuroplastic nature is a powerful reminder that change is always possible. Cognitive distortions, though deeply ingrained, are not permanent. With consistent effort through techniques like CBT, mindfulness, and emotional regulation, individuals can reshape their brains to respond more adaptively, fostering clarity, balance, and emotional well-being.

Key Takeaways

1.Neuroplasticity *provides the biological foundation for therapies like CBT, enabling the brain to adapt and grow through new experiences.*

2.Cognitive restructuring *strengthens healthier neural pathways while weakening those tied to distorted thinking.*

3.Practices like mindfulness *and graded exposure therapy enhance PFC activity and reduce amygdala hyperactivity, fostering emotional resilience.*

By understanding and leveraging neuroplasticity, individuals can transform their thought patterns, replacing distortion-driven responses with healthier, more balanced perspectives.

• • •

Epigenetics, Thinking, and Cognitive Distortions

The way we think and the cognitive distortions we experience are not solely shaped by our immediate environment or life experiences. Recent advances in **epigenetics**—*the study of how environmental factors can influence gene expression—shed light on the complex interplay between biology, behavior, and thought patterns. This emerging field reveals that our genetic blueprint is more flexible than previously believed, and our mental health, including the tendency toward distorted thinking, can be influenced by both inherited and environmental factors.*

What Is Epigenetics?

Epigenetics explores how genes can be turned "on" or "off" by environmental stimuli, including stress, trauma, diet, and even social interactions. Unlike changes to the DNA sequence itself, epigenetic changes are reversible and can affect how we respond to our environment.

Key Concepts in Epigenetics:

Gene Expression:

Epigenetic mechanisms, such as DNA methylation and histone modification, regulate whether specific genes are active or silent.

Intergenerational Influence:

Epigenetic changes triggered by life experiences, such as trauma or chronic stress, can be passed down to subsequent generations, influencing their susceptibility to cognitive distortions and emotional challenges.

How Epigenetics Influences Thinking and Cognitive Distortions

1. Stress and Gene Activation

Chronic stress can activate genes that heighten emotional reactivity, increasing susceptibility to cognitive distortions like catastrophizing and emotional reasoning.

Research Insight: *A landmark study by Yehuda et al. (2005) on Holocaust survivors and their descendants revealed that traumatic experiences could alter the expression of stress-related genes, predisposing* *future generations to anxiety and distorted thinking.*

2. Trauma and Overgeneralization

Traumatic events can leave epigenetic marks that sensitize the brain's fear circuitry, particularly the amygdala, leading to exaggerated responses and distortions like overgeneralization.

Example: *A person whose ancestors experienced famine may overgeneralize small setbacks into broader fears of deprivation or failure.*

3. Early Life Experiences and Attachment

The quality of caregiving in early childhood can influence epigenetic mechanisms that shape the brain's emotional regulation centers, such as the prefrontal cortex and hippocampus. These changes can predispose individuals to anxious or avoidant attachment styles, which are linked to distortions like mind reading and personalization.

Research Insight: *McGowan et al. (2009) found that adults who experienced childhood abuse had altered epigenetic markers on genes associated with stress regulation, increasing vulnerability to negative thought patterns.*

Positive Epigenetic Changes: Rewiring Through Thought

The brain's epigenetic flexibility means that positive experiences, behaviors, and thought patterns can create beneficial changes at the genetic level. Practices like mindfulness, cognitive behavioral therapy (CBT), and even gratitude journaling have been shown to reverse some of the epigenetic effects of stress and trauma.

Research Insight: *Studies by Kaliman et al. (2014) revealed that mindfulness meditation altered epigenetic markers linked to inflammation and stress, promoting a more balanced emotional state.*

Gratitude and Resilience:

Gratitude *practices influence epigenetic markers associated with dopamine production, fostering positive thinking and reducing distortions like mental filtering.*

Epigenetics and Cognitive Distortions: The Bigger Picture

Epigenetics demonstrates that while we may inherit certain predispositions to distorted thinking, these tendencies are not set in stone. By understanding the biological and environmental factors at play, we can take proactive steps to rewire our thought patterns and create a more positive, resilient mental framework.

This intersection of epigenetics, thinking, and cognitive distortions reinforces a hopeful message: our brains and thoughts are not only adaptable but also deeply influenced by the choices we make and the environments we cultivate.

Conclusion: The Interplay of Thinking Styles and Biology

Understanding how different thinking types interact with the brain's anatomy and unconscious processes sheds light on the origins of cognitive distortions. While these patterns may feel automatic, they are not permanent. By cultivating awareness of our thinking style and leveraging neuroplasticity, we can rewire our brains for healthier, more balanced thought patterns.

• • •

• • •

CHAPTER III

Types of Cognitive Distortions

Imagine looking at life through a warped mirror. What you see isn't a true reflection but a distorted version of reality. This is the essence of cognitive distortions—mental shortcuts and biases that twist our perceptions, leading to irrational and often self-defeating thoughts.

Cognitive distortions are not rare; they're universal. Everyone experiences them, whether it's jumping to conclusions, fixating on the negative, or catastrophizing about the future. These thought patterns are automatic and deeply ingrained, often shaping our emotions and behaviors without us even realizing it.

In this chapter, we'll explore the most common types of cognitive distortions, understand how they influence our thinking, and uncover the psychological mechanisms that keep them alive. By identifying these mental traps, we take the first step toward breaking free from their grip and fostering healthier, more balanced thought patterns.

Here's a closer look at the most common types of cognitive distortions:

1.All-or-Nothing Thinking

"If I'm not perfect, I've failed."

The World in Black and White

Imagine a student who receives an 85% on an exam. Most people would view this as a solid performance. But for someone caught in the trap of all-or-nothing thinking, the reaction might be starkly different:

"I didn't get 100%. I've failed."

"If I can't be the best, what's the point?"

All-or-nothing thinking, also known as black-and-white thinking, is the distortion that reduces the complexity of life into two extremes. You're either a success or a failure. Right or wrong. Good or bad. There's no room for nuance, no space for the shades of gray that make up most of human experience.

This type of thinking is particularly common in perfectionists, but it can affect anyone. At its core, it's a rigid and unforgiving way of interpreting events—and it often leads to feelings of frustration, inadequacy, and burnout.

Spotting All-or-Nothing Thinking in Your Life

This distortion can manifest in countless ways, from how you evaluate yourself to how you judge others or situations. Here are some common examples:

1.

Personal Performance:

"If I make one mistake, the entire project is ruined."

"I didn't finish my workout, so it was a waste of time."

1.

Relationships:

"If my partner truly loved me, they'd always understand me."

"They forgot my birthday—they're a terrible friend."

1.

Self-Identity:

"I'm either a success or a failure. There's no in-between."

"If I can't handle this, I'm weak."

Sound familiar? If so, you're not alone. All-or-nothing thinking is one of the most common cognitive distortions, and its effects can be deeply damaging—both to our self-esteem and our relationships.

Why We Think in Extremes

The roots of all-or-nothing thinking lie in our brain's natural tendency to simplify complex information. Nuance requires effort. It takes time and energy to hold competing ideas in mind, weigh evidence, and see the big picture.

*When faced with stress or uncertainty, our brains often take shortcuts. These shortcuts, known as **cognitive heuristics**, make decision-making faster but less accurate. Black-and-white thinking is one such shortcut—it offers clarity and certainty, even if it's based on flawed logic.*

In addition, many of us grow up in environments that reward all-or-nothing thinking. Phrases like "If you're not first, you're last" or "Go big or go home" reflect a cultural tendency to view success and failure as absolutes. Over time, these messages can become internalized, shaping how we see ourselves and the world.

The Cost of All-or-Nothing Thinking

At first glance, all-or-nothing thinking might seem like a motivator. After all, aiming for perfection pushes us to achieve great things, right? But in reality, this distortion often backfires.

1.Paralysis and Procrastination:

If you believe that anything less than perfection is unacceptable, you might avoid starting tasks altogether. Why bother if you can't guarantee success?

2.Emotional Turmoil:

Viewing setbacks as failures can lead to feelings of inadequacy, shame, and hopelessness.

3.Strained Relationships:

Expecting others to meet impossible standards—or judging them harshly for minor mistakes—can create unnecessary conflict.

4.Burnout:

Pushing yourself to achieve perfection in every area of life is exhausting and unsustainable.

Breaking Free from Black-and-White Thinking

The good news is that all-or-nothing thinking is a habit—and like any habit, it can be changed. Here are practical strategies to help you move toward more balanced and flexible thinking:

1. Challenge the Extremes:
When you catch yourself thinking in absolutes, pause and ask:

"Is this really true?"

"What evidence supports this thought? What evidence contradicts it?"

For example:

Thought: "I failed because I didn't finish everything on my to-do list."

Challenge: "Did I really fail? Or did I succeed in completing some tasks, even if not all of them?"

2. Find the Middle Ground:
Force yourself to identify the "gray area" between two extremes.

Instead of "I'm either a success or a failure," try "I'm making progress, even if I'm not where I want to be yet."

Instead of "They're a perfect partner or a terrible one," try "They're human—they have strengths and flaws, just like me."

3. Reframe Mistakes as Learning Opportunities:
Perfection doesn't exist. Mistakes are not failures; they're opportunities to grow.

Instead of "I failed the presentation," try "I learned how to improve for next time."

4. Use "And" Instead of "Or":
Replace either/or thinking with both/and thinking.

"I can feel disappointed and proud of the effort I put in."

"I can value independence and ask for help when I need it."

5. Practice Self-Compassion:
When you catch yourself falling into all-or-nothing thinking, take a moment to be kind to yourself. Remind yourself that imperfection is not a flaw—it's part of being human.

Case Study: Rewriting the Narrative

Let's revisit the student who received an 85% on their exam. Here's how they might reframe their all-or-nothing thoughts:

Initial Thought: "I didn't get 100%. I've failed."

Reframed Thought: "85% is a strong score. I can be proud of my effort while still aiming to improve next time."

This small shift in perspective can make a world of difference—not just in how the student feels about their grade, but in how they approach future challenges.

Moving Forward

All-or-nothing thinking is powerful, but so is your ability to change. Each time you challenge a black-and-white thought, you're rewiring your brain, creating new pathways for balanced and flexible thinking. Over time, these small shifts can lead to profound transformation.

*In the next chapter, we'll dive into another common distortion: **Overgeneralization**—the tendency to turn one negative event into a sweeping conclusion about yourself or your life.*

Let's keep unraveling the patterns that hold us back, one distortion at a time.

<u>2. Overgeneralization</u>

"Why does this always happen to me?"

The Trap of Sweeping Conclusions

Picture this: You're running late for an important meeting, and as you rush out the door, you spill coffee on your shirt. Embarrassed and frustrated, you mutter to yourself:

"I can't believe this. I always screw things up."

"Nothing ever goes right for me."

What just happened? A single event—a spilled cup of coffee—has been turned into a grand statement about your abilities and your life. This is **overgeneralization**, *the cognitive distortion that takes one isolated incident and applies it broadly, as though it defines a pattern or rule.*

What Is Overgeneralization?

Overgeneralization occurs when we take a single negative experience and assume it's representative of all future experiences or our overall worth. It's like looking at one raindrop and concluding that it will rain forever.

This type of thinking can feel convincing, even logical, because our brains are wired to look for patterns. In reality, overgeneralization blinds us to nuance, possibility, and change.

How Overgeneralization Shows Up in Life

Overgeneralization can creep into every corner of our thinking, shaping how we view ourselves, others, and the world. Here are some examples:

1. Self-Esteem:

"I didn't get the job I wanted. I'll never succeed in my career."

"I forgot to call my friend back. I'm such a terrible person."

2. Relationships:

"They didn't text me back right away. Nobody really cares about me."

"My last relationship ended badly. I'm destined to be alone forever."

3. Worldview:

"I failed this one test. I'm just not smart enough for school."

"If one person betrayed me, I can't trust anyone."

Overgeneralization often uses words like always, never, everyone, or no one, making sweeping statements that leave no room for exceptions or complexity.

Why We Overgeneralize

At its core, overgeneralization is a defense mechanism. By assuming the worst, we try to protect ourselves from future pain or disappointment. If you believe, "Nothing ever works out for me," you might avoid taking risks—thinking it's better to stay safe than face another potential failure.

Overgeneralization can also be fueled by strong emotions, particularly sadness or anxiety. When we feel overwhelmed, our thinking becomes rigid, and it's easier to see one setback as evidence of a broader truth.

The Cost of Overgeneralization

While this distortion might seem like a way to shield yourself from hurt, it often causes more harm than good.

1.Low Self-Worth:

Constantly labeling yourself as a failure or unworthy can erode confidence and motivation.

2.Missed Opportunities:

Assuming you'll always fail may stop you from trying new things or pursuing your goals.

3.Strained Relationships:

Generalizing one person's actions as a reflection of everyone's intentions can lead to mistrust and isolation.

4.Hopelessness:

Believing that "nothing ever changes" can make you feel stuck and powerless.

Breaking Free from Overgeneralization

Overgeneralization thrives on habit and repetition, but with practice, you can learn to interrupt and challenge these patterns. Here's how:

1. Look for the Exceptions:

Overgeneralization relies on ignoring evidence that contradicts the sweeping statement. Force yourself to find exceptions.

Thought: "I always mess up at work."

Challenge: "Actually, I handled last week's project really well. One mistake doesn't mean I always mess up."

2. Use Precise Language:

Words like always and never are rarely true. Replace them with more accurate, specific phrasing.

Thought: "Nothing ever works out for me."

Reframe: "This one situation didn't go as planned, but that doesn't mean other things won't work out."

3. Zoom Out:

When you feel stuck in a pattern, step back and consider the bigger picture.

Ask yourself: "Is this really the whole story, or am I focusing on one part of it?"

4. Challenge the Underlying Belief:

Overgeneralization often stems from deeper insecurities. Explore the root of the belief and test its validity.

Belief: "I'm unlovable because my last relationship ended badly."

Reframe: "One relationship didn't work out, but that doesn't mean I'm unlovable. Many people have fulfilling relationships after setbacks."

5. Keep a Success Log:
Write down examples of times when things went well for you. When overgeneralization strikes, revisit your log to remind yourself that failure is not your default setting.

Case Study: Overgeneralization in Action

The Situation:
Maria, a 29-year-old graphic designer, submits a project to her client, only to receive critical feedback. Disheartened, she thinks:

"I'll never be good at my job. Clients will always hate my work."

The Challenge:
Maria's therapist helps her break down her thought:

Is it true that all her clients hate her work? No—this client had some criticisms, but others have been satisfied.

Does one critical review mean she'll never succeed? No—feedback is an opportunity to improve, not a final judgment on her talent.

The Reframe:
Maria replaces her thought with: "This feedback is tough to hear, but it's one project, not my entire career. I can use this as a learning opportunity to grow."

Moving Forward

Overgeneralization is like looking at life through a narrow lens, seeing only the negative and ignoring the rest. By challenging this distortion, you can widen your perspective and see the full picture—the struggles and successes, setbacks and growth.

*In the next chapter, we'll tackle **Mental Filtering**, the distortion that makes you focus exclusively on the negative while dismissing the positive. If you've ever felt like one bad moment overshadowed an entire day, this chapter is for you.*

<u>3.Mental Filtering</u>

"Why do I only see the bad?"

The Power of Focus

Picture this: You're giving a presentation at work. Afterward, you receive feedback from your colleagues: ten glowing compliments and one mildly critical comment. That evening, as you replay the day in your mind, what sticks out?

For many of us, it's not the praise or the recognition. It's that one negative remark—a tiny blemish on an otherwise successful day.

*This is **mental filtering**, a cognitive distortion where you zero in on the negative aspects of an experience while completely ignoring the positive ones. It's like looking at a beautiful sunset but only focusing on a single dark cloud in the sky.*

What Is Mental Filtering?

Mental filtering occurs when you allow one negative detail to overshadow an entire experience. Even if the positive far outweighs the negative, this distortion makes it difficult to see the good.

It's not that positive events don't exist—they're just filtered out, leaving a skewed and incomplete version of reality.

How Mental Filtering Impacts Life

This distortion can affect your emotions, your self-esteem, and your relationships. Here's how it often manifests:

1.In Self-Evaluation:

"I made one mistake during my presentation. I'm terrible at public speaking."

"My boss didn't say anything about my report. They must have hated it."

2.In Relationships:

"My partner forgot to thank me for cooking dinner. They don't appreciate me at all."

"My friend didn't call me back today. They must not care about our friendship."

3.In Life Overall:

"I had a flat tire on my way to work. Today is ruined."

"I didn't win the award I applied for. All my hard work was pointless."

Why Do We Focus on the Negative?

Mental filtering is rooted in our brain's negativity bias—a survival mechanism that evolved to help us focus on threats and dangers. For our ancestors, overlooking a rustle in the bushes could mean death, so the brain developed a tendency to prioritize negative stimuli.

While this bias was useful in prehistoric times, it can be counterproductive in modern life. Instead of keeping us safe, it often keeps us stuck in a cycle of negative thinking, eroding our happiness and resilience.

The Consequences of Mental Filtering

The effects of mental filtering can be profound and far-reaching:

1.Low Self-Esteem:

Constantly focusing on your flaws or mistakes can make you feel unworthy or incapable.

2.Chronic Stress and Anxiety:

Overemphasizing negatives creates a distorted sense of danger or failure, leaving you in a constant state of worry.

3.Strained Relationships:

Focusing on a partner's shortcomings while ignoring their positive traits can lead to resentment and conflict.

4.Missed Joy:

When you're stuck in mental filtering, you miss out on life's many small victories and moments of happiness.

How to Break Free from Mental Filtering

Fortunately, mental filtering is not a permanent mindset. With practice, you can learn to see the full picture—both the challenges and the blessings. Here are some steps to help you overcome this distortion:

1. Actively Seek the Positive:
When you catch yourself focusing on the negative, challenge yourself to identify at least three positive aspects of the situation.

Example: "I messed up one slide during my presentation."

Positive Counterpoints: "Most of the presentation went smoothly. I prepared thoroughly. People seemed engaged and asked thoughtful questions."

2. Balance the Narrative:
Write down the event or situation in a journal. Next, divide the page into two columns:

In one column, list the negative aspects.

In the other, list the positive aspects.

This exercise forces you to confront the reality that even challenging situations have upsides.

3. Challenge the Filter:
Ask yourself:

"Am I ignoring evidence that contradicts my negative focus?"

"What would a more balanced perspective look like?"

4. Keep a Gratitude Log:
At the end of each day, write down three things you're grateful for. This simple practice trains your brain to notice the positives and can gradually rewire your thought patterns.

5. Seek Feedback:
If you're unsure whether you're viewing a situation accurately, ask a trusted friend or colleague for their perspective. Their input can help you see what you might be missing.

Case Study: Seeing the Full Picture

The Situation:
Arjun, a 40-year-old teacher, receives feedback on his lesson plan. Out of 20 comments, 18 are positive, and

2 suggest areas for improvement. Instead of feeling encouraged, Arjun fixates on the two critiques.

The Challenge:
Arjun's mentor notices his disappointment and helps him reflect:

"What do the positive comments say about your teaching?"

"What can you learn from the critical feedback?"

The Reframe:
Arjun realizes the positives outweigh the negatives. He reframes his thinking: "The feedback shows that I'm doing a lot right, and the critiques give me an opportunity to grow."

Moving Forward

Mental filtering can feel automatic and overwhelming, but with practice, you can retrain your mind to focus on the full picture. Life is rarely all good or all bad—it's a complex, colorful tapestry of experiences. By learning to see the good along with the challenges, you can build resilience, gratitude, and a more balanced perspective.

In the next chapter, we'll explore **Catastrophizing**—*the distortion that turns small problems into imagined disasters. If you've ever spiraled into "what-if" scenarios, stay tuned.*

4.Catastrophizing

"What if everything goes wrong?"

The Spiral of Worst-Case Scenarios

Imagine this: Your boss asks to meet with you unexpectedly. Your mind immediately races:

"What if I made a huge mistake?"

"What if I lose my job?"

"What if I can't pay my bills? I could lose my house. My whole life will fall apart."

*This is **catastrophizing**, a cognitive distortion that turns small concerns into overwhelming disasters. It's the mental equivalent of tripping on a crack in the sidewalk and imagining yourself plummeting off a cliff.*

Catastrophizing isn't just stressful—it's exhausting. It hijacks your emotional well-being, pulling you into a cycle of fear and helplessness over events that may never even happen.

What Is Catastrophizing?

At its core, catastrophizing is the tendency to anticipate the worst possible outcome in any given situation, regardless of how unlikely it is. This distortion involves two key elements:

1.Exaggeration:

Turning a small problem into a monumental crisis.

Example: "I failed one test; I'm going to fail the entire course."

2.Assuming the Worst:

Jumping to conclusions about negative outcomes.

Example: "The doctor wants to run more tests—what if I have a terminal illness?"

Catastrophizing thrives on uncertainty, turning the unknown into a breeding ground for anxiety and fear.

How Catastrophizing Impacts Life

This distortion can significantly affect your emotional and physical health, as well as your relationships and decision-making.

Emotional Strain:

Constantly imagining worst-case scenarios can lead to chronic stress, anxiety, and feelings of powerlessness.

Inaction:

Overwhelmed by imagined disasters, you may avoid taking risks or pursuing opportunities.

Strained Relationships:

Catastrophizing can lead to excessive worry over loved ones, creating tension and frustration.

Physical Health:

Prolonged stress from catastrophizing can take a toll on your body, contributing to headaches, insomnia, and other stress-related conditions.

Why We Catastrophize

Catastrophizing often stems from a natural desire to prepare for danger. By imagining worst-case scenarios, our minds attempt to protect us from potential harm. However, this survival mechanism can backfire when applied to everyday situations.

Other contributing factors include:

Past Experiences:

If something went wrong before, your brain may assume it will happen again.

Perfectionism:

Fear of failure can lead to imagining extreme consequences for even minor mistakes.

Uncertainty Intolerance:

If you struggle with uncertainty, catastrophizing offers the illusion of control by mentally preparing for every possible outcome.

Breaking the Cycle of Catastrophizing

Catastrophizing is a mental habit, and like any habit, it can be changed with awareness and practice. Here's how:

1. Separate Fact from Fiction:
When you notice yourself spiraling into worst-case scenarios, pause and ask:

"What is the evidence that this will happen?"

"Am I basing this thought on facts or fears?"

Write down your concerns and evaluate them logically. Often, you'll find that the worst-case scenario is far less likely than it feels.

2. Focus on the Present Moment:
Catastrophizing thrives on imagining the future. Ground yourself in the present by using mindfulness

techniques:

Take deep breaths and describe your surroundings.

Remind yourself: "Right now, I am safe, and nothing bad is happening."

3. Create a Plan, Not a Panic:
If you're worried about a specific outcome, shift your energy from catastrophizing to problem-solving.

Concern: "What if I fail this exam?"

Plan: "I'll create a study schedule and ask for help if I need it. If I don't pass, I'll look into retaking it."

Having a concrete plan can reduce feelings of helplessness and anxiety.

4. Play It Out to the End:
Sometimes, the best way to disarm a worst-case scenario is to imagine it fully—and then realize you could handle it.

Question: "If the worst did happen, what would I do?"

Example: "If I lost my job, I could update my résumé, apply for new positions, and reach out to my network for support."

Realizing your own resilience can help put fears into perspective.

5. Use a Counterbalance Thought:
Replace catastrophic thoughts with more balanced, realistic ones.

Thought: "If I mess up this presentation, I'll lose my job."

Counterbalance: "Mistakes happen to everyone. One presentation won't define my entire career."

Case Study: Turning Catastrophe into Calm

The Situation:
Priya, a 27-year-old marketing executive, is asked to present a new campaign idea to her team. As the meeting approaches, she begins to spiral:

"What if they hate my ideas?"

"What if I embarrass myself? They'll think I'm incompetent. I might even get fired."

The Challenge:
Priya works with a coach to examine her thoughts:

Evidence: "Have I done good work in the past?" Yes.

Likelihood: "Is it realistic that one bad meeting would lead to being fired?" No.

The Reframe:
Priya replaces her catastrophic thoughts with: "I've prepared thoroughly. Even if my ideas aren't perfect, this is a chance to get valuable feedback and grow."

When the day arrives, Priya delivers her presentation confidently—and her team's constructive input helps her improve her campaign.

Moving Forward

Catastrophizing can feel overwhelming, but it's important to remember that your thoughts are not facts. By challenging worst-case scenarios and focusing on the present moment, you can break free from the cycle of fear and reclaim your emotional balance.

*In the next chapter, we'll explore **Personalization**, the distortion that makes you take responsibility for things that aren't yours to bear. If you've ever thought, "It's all my fault," this chapter is for you.*

5.Personalization

"Why do I blame myself for everything?"

The Burden of Over-Responsibility

Imagine this: A friend seems distant during your conversation, giving one-word replies and avoiding eye contact. Instead of considering other possibilities, your mind leaps to one conclusion:

"I must have said something wrong."

"It's my fault they're upset."

This is **personalization**, *the cognitive distortion that makes you take responsibility for events or situations that are not entirely—or even remotely—under your control.*

When caught in the trap of personalization, every problem feels like your fault, and every negative outcome becomes a reflection of your worth. It's like carrying a weight that doesn't belong to you, one that you were never meant to bear.

What Is Personalization?

Personalization occurs when you assume responsibility for external events, regardless of the actual cause. This distortion often involves interpreting other people's emotions or actions as being directly related to you.

Two key elements define personalization:

1.Excessive Responsibility:

Believing you are responsible for things beyond your control.

Example: "My friend didn't get the promotion—if only I had helped them more with their résumé."

2.Self-Blame:

Viewing yourself as the cause of others' problems or negative emotions.

Example: "The dinner party was awkward because I didn't keep the conversation going."

How Personalization Shows Up in Life

Personalization can seep into various aspects of life, often without you realizing it:

In Relationships:

"My partner seems upset—it must be something I did."

"If my child is struggling in school, it's because I'm a bad parent."

At Work:

"The project didn't succeed because I wasn't good enough."

"If my colleague is stressed, I must not be doing enough to help."

In Everyday Interactions:

"That stranger didn't smile back at me—I must look unapproachable."

"The weather ruined our picnic. I should have picked a better day."

Personalization often goes hand-in-hand with guilt and feelings of inadequacy, reinforcing a cycle of negative self-talk.

Why We Personalize

Personalization often stems from deeply ingrained beliefs and habits, including:

Desire for Control:

Taking responsibility can create the illusion of control in chaotic situations. If you're at fault, you believe you can fix it.

Empathy Turned Inward:

Highly empathetic individuals may internalize others' struggles, confusing compassion with blame.

Past Conditioning:

If you grew up in an environment where blame was often placed on you, personalization can become a default response.

The Cost of Personalization

While taking responsibility can be a sign of maturity, excessive personalization can be harmful.

1.Emotional Burnout:

Carrying blame for things outside your control can lead to chronic stress and exhaustion.

2.Erosion of Self-Worth:

Viewing yourself as the source of every problem reinforces feelings of inadequacy and self-doubt.

3.Strained Relationships:

Constantly assuming blame can create imbalanced dynamics, where you over-apologize or take on burdens that aren't yours.

4.Missed Opportunities for Growth:

By focusing solely on your role, you may overlook other factors that contribute to a situation—and miss the chance to address them.

Breaking Free from Personalization

Overcoming personalization requires a shift in perspective, from self-blame to shared understanding. Here's how:

1. Identify What's Within Your Control:
Ask yourself:

"What part of this situation am I actually responsible for?"

"What factors are outside my control?"

Recognizing the limits of your responsibility can help you focus on what you can influence—without carrying unnecessary guilt.

2. Consider Alternative Explanations:

When you notice yourself personalizing, pause and ask:

"Could there be another reason for this situation?"

"What evidence supports my assumption? What contradicts it?"

For example:

Thought: "My friend didn't reply to my text—they must be upset with me."

Reframe: "Maybe they're busy or having a tough day."

3. Practice Emotional Detachment:

It's important to empathize with others without absorbing their emotions.

Remind yourself: "I can care about their feelings without taking responsibility for them."

4. Use Balanced Language:

Replace self-blaming thoughts with more balanced statements.

Thought: "I ruined the dinner party because I wasn't engaging enough."

Reframe: "The conversation felt awkward at times, but it wasn't entirely my responsibility."

5. Reflect on Patterns of Blame:
Think back to situations where you personalized unnecessarily. Write down what actually caused the issue and how much control you realistically had. Over time, this exercise can help you identify and challenge personalization more quickly.

Case Study: Letting Go of Unnecessary Blame

The Situation:
James, a 35-year-old project manager, notices that his colleague Sarah has been quiet in meetings. He assumes it's because she's upset with him for not taking her suggestion in the last project discussion.

The Challenge:
James personalizes the situation, blaming himself without evidence. With the help of a coach, he examines the facts:

Has Sarah said she's upset? No.

Could there be other reasons for her behavior? Yes—she might be busy or distracted.

The Reframe:
James reminds himself: "Sarah's mood might have nothing to do with me. If she wants to share something, she will. Until then, I'll focus on our work together."

This shift allows James to let go of unnecessary guilt and approach the situation with clarity and confidence.

Moving Forward

Personalization often feels like a reflex, but it's a habit you can change. By recognizing what's within your control—and what isn't—you can free yourself from the weight of unnecessary blame.

In the next chapter, we'll tackle **Emotional Reasoning**, *the distortion that makes you believe your feelings are facts. If you've ever thought, "I feel it, so it must be true," this chapter will help you regain clarity and perspective.*

6.Emotional Reasoning

"I feel it, so it must be true."

The Trap of Feelings-as-Facts

Imagine this: You're preparing to give a speech in front of a crowd. As you stand backstage, your heart races, your palms sweat, and a wave of doubt washes over you. A thought emerges:

"I feel unprepared. I must not be ready for this."

Or perhaps, after a tense conversation with a friend, you think:

"I feel hurt, so they must have meant to upset me."

This is **emotional reasoning**, the cognitive distortion that treats feelings as evidence of truth. It's the mental shortcut that says:

If I feel afraid, there must be danger.

If I feel inadequate, I must be incapable.

If I feel unloved, no one cares about me.

While emotions are powerful and deeply informative, they are not always accurate reflections of reality. Emotional reasoning blurs the line between subjective feelings and objective facts, leading to skewed perceptions of yourself, others, and the world.

What Is Emotional Reasoning?

Emotional reasoning occurs when you interpret situations based solely on how you feel, rather than considering other evidence. It's like looking at the world through tinted glasses, where everything is colored by your current emotional state.

Common patterns of emotional reasoning include:

Fear Equals Danger:

"I feel anxious about traveling, so it must not be safe."

Guilt Equals Responsibility:

"I feel guilty, so I must have done something wrong."

Inadequacy Equals Failure:

"I feel like I'm not good enough, so I must be a failure."

Emotional reasoning can be particularly sneaky because it feels intuitive. After all, emotions are real, vivid, and immediate. But they are not facts—they are signals, influenced by past experiences, current stressors, and even physical states like hunger or fatigue.

How Emotional Reasoning Impacts Life

When unchecked, emotional reasoning can lead to:

Self-Doubt:

Believing your negative feelings define your abilities or worth.

Poor Decision-Making:

Avoiding opportunities because of fear or self-doubt, even when the risks are low.

Misunderstandings in Relationships:

Assuming others' intentions based on your emotional reactions rather than their actual behavior.

Chronic Stress and Anxiety:

Amplifying feelings of danger or failure, even in low-stakes situations.

Why Do We Rely on Emotional Reasoning?

Emotional reasoning stems from the brain's reliance on emotions as quick, instinctive guides for decision-making. In the past, feeling afraid likely meant there was a predator nearby, and acting on that fear increased the chances of survival.

In today's world, emotions are still powerful signals, but they're often influenced by factors unrelated to the immediate situation:

Past Experiences: *Emotional wounds or traumas can color current perceptions.*

Social Conditioning: *Feeling guilty or inadequate may reflect societal pressures rather than personal failings.*

Biology: *Hormonal shifts, lack of sleep, or even hunger can amplify emotions.*

While emotions can provide valuable insight, relying on them as your sole guide can lead to distorted thinking and unnecessary suffering.

Breaking Free from Emotional Reasoning

Overcoming emotional reasoning involves separating feelings from facts and learning to question the assumptions behind your emotions. Here's how:

1. Pause and Label the Emotion:
When you notice emotional reasoning, take a step back and identify what you're feeling.

"I'm feeling anxious."

"I'm feeling hurt."

Labeling the emotion creates distance, allowing you to observe it without being consumed by it.

2. Ask for Evidence:
Challenge the assumption that your feelings are facts. Ask yourself:

"What evidence supports this thought?"

"What evidence contradicts it?"

For example:

Thought: "I feel like I'm going to fail this test."

Evidence: "I've studied consistently, and I understand the material."

3. Recognize the Temporary Nature of Emotions:
Remind yourself that emotions are fleeting—they rise and fall like waves. Just because you feel something strongly now doesn't mean it will last or that it's true.

4. Balance Feelings with Logic:
Replace emotion-driven thoughts with balanced, fact-based ones.

Thought: "I feel unlovable, so no one cares about me."

Reframe: "Feeling lonely doesn't mean I'm unlovable. My friends and family care about me, even if I don't feel it right now."

5. Use the Observer Perspective:
Imagine how someone else might view the situation. What would a friend or mentor say? This shift can help you see beyond your immediate emotional response.

Case Study: Challenging Emotional Reasoning

The Situation:
Nina, a 32-year-old artist, submits her portfolio for a gallery exhibition. A week later, she hasn't heard back. She begins to think:

"I feel like they hated my work. I must not be talented enough."

The Challenge:
Nina works through the following steps:

1.Label the Emotion: "I feel insecure and anxious."

2.Examine the Evidence: "Have I received positive feedback on my work before? Yes. Is it possible they're still reviewing submissions? Yes."

3.Reframe the Thought: "Feeling anxious doesn't mean I'm untalented. The delay could be unrelated to me."

By separating her feelings from reality, Nina avoids spiraling into self-doubt and continues creating new art.

Moving Forward

Emotions are valuable guides, but they are not infallible. By learning to question the assumptions behind emotional reasoning, you can respond to situations with greater clarity, balance, and confidence.

*In the next chapter, we'll explore **Should Statements**, the distortion that turns rigid expectations into a source of guilt and frustration. If you've ever felt* *trapped by "shoulds" and "musts," this chapter will help you break free.*

7.Should Statements

"Trapped by Expectations."

The Weight of the Word 'Should'

Have you ever said to yourself:

"I should be more productive."

"I must always make everyone happy."

"I ought to have achieved more by now."

These phrases might seem harmless, even motivating. But for many people, they're heavy chains of self-imposed expectations, pulling them into cycles of guilt, frustration, and self-doubt.

Should statements *are a cognitive distortion that involves holding yourself—or others—to rigid, unrealistic standards. They focus on what "ought" to be, rather than accepting what is, creating a constant sense of dissatisfaction and failure.*

What Are Should Statements?

Should statements occur when you use words like should, must, or ought to to impose strict rules or expectations on yourself, others, or the world. These statements are usually unrealistic, inflexible, and emotionally draining.

They often sound like:

Self-Directed Shoulds:

"I should exercise every day, or I'm lazy."

"I must be the perfect parent, or I'm failing."

Other-Directed Shoulds:

"They should know how I feel without me saying it."

"He must call me every day if he really cares."

World-Directed Shoulds:

"Life ought to be fair."

"This kind of thing shouldn't happen to me."

While it's natural to have goals and values, should statements turn aspirations into harsh judgments, leaving no room for flexibility or forgiveness.

How Should Statements Impact Life

Should statements are deceptively harmful. They might appear as motivational tools, but in reality, they:

Erode Self-Worth:

Constantly failing to meet impossible standards reinforces feelings of inadequacy.

Fuel Resentment in Relationships:

Expecting others to follow your internal "rules" can lead to frustration when they don't comply.

Create Chronic Stress:

Feeling like you're always falling short or that others are failing you can lead to anxiety and burnout.

Distort Reality:

Focusing on how things "should" be blinds you to how they actually are, preventing acceptance and growth.

Why Do We Use Should Statements?

Should statements often stem from internalized beliefs and societal pressures:

Cultural and Family Expectations:

Growing up with strict rules about success, behavior, or appearance can create lifelong should-based thinking.

Perfectionism:

Striving for an idealized version of yourself often leads to unrealistic expectations.

Desire for Control:

Should statements impose a sense of order on an unpredictable world, even if the control is illusory.

Breaking Free from Should Statements

Overcoming should-based thinking involves shifting from rigid expectations to more compassionate and realistic perspectives. Here's how:

1. Identify Your Should Statements:
Start by noticing when you use the words should, must, or ought to. Pay attention to how these thoughts make you feel—do they motivate you, or do they create guilt and frustration?

Example: "I should be more productive."

Emotional Impact: Guilt, stress, and a sense of failure.

2. Challenge the Should:
Ask yourself:

"Is this expectation realistic or helpful?"

"Who says I should do this? Where does this rule come from?"

Replace harsh shoulds with more balanced statements:

Original: "I should always be available for my friends."

Reframe: "I value supporting my friends, but it's okay to set boundaries when I need to rest."

3. Replace Should with Want or Could:
Shifting your language can change how you perceive your goals and choices.

Instead of: "I should go to the gym today."

Try: "I want to go to the gym because it helps me feel healthy."

Or: "I could go to the gym, but it's also okay to rest if I need to."

4. Embrace Flexibility and Self-Compassion:
Life is rarely black-and-white. Allow yourself to adapt

to changing circumstances without judgment.

Example: "I didn't finish my to-do list today, and that's okay. I can try again tomorrow."

5. Let Go of Unrealistic Expectations for Others: *Recognize that you can't control other people's actions or meet all their needs. Shift from rigid rules to open communication.*

Instead of: "They should know how I feel."

Reframe: "It would be helpful if they understood how I feel. I'll share my perspective with them."

Case Study: Rewriting the Rules

The Situation:

Aria, a 38-year-old working mother, constantly tells herself:

"I should be able to handle everything."

"I must never let my family see me struggle."

These thoughts leave her feeling exhausted and inadequate.

The Challenge:

Aria begins to notice the toll of her should statements. With the help of a therapist, she questions their origins:

"Where did I learn that struggling is unacceptable?"

"Does meeting every expectation make me a better mother, or just a more stressed one?"

The Reframe:

Aria replaces her should statements with compassionate alternatives:

"I'm doing my best, and it's okay to ask for help."

"Struggling doesn't make me a bad parent—it makes me human."

This shift allows Aria to let go of guilt and prioritize her well-being, improving both her life and her relationships.

Moving Forward

Should statements are like invisible rules that dictate how we "ought" to live—but you have the power to rewrite them. By replacing rigid expectations with self-compassion and flexibility, you can free yourself from the cycle of guilt and frustration.

In the next chapter, we'll tackle **Mind Reading and Fortune-Telling**, *the distortions that make us believe we know what others are thinking or that we can predict the future. If you've ever thought, "I know they're judging me," this chapter will help you find clarity.*

8.Mind Reading and Fortune-Telling

"Assuming the Worst"

When Your Mind Plays Tricks on You

Imagine this: You walk into a room, and a group of colleagues stops talking. Immediately, your thoughts spiral:

"They were talking about me."

"They probably think I'm incompetent."

Or perhaps you're preparing for a big presentation, and your mind races ahead:

"I just know I'm going to mess this up."

"The audience will hate it. They'll think I have no idea what I'm doing."

*These are examples of **mind reading** and **fortune-telling**, two closely related cognitive distortions. In both cases, your mind fills in the gaps with* assumptions—often negative ones—about what others think or what the future holds.

The problem? These assumptions feel so real that they shape your emotions and behavior, even though they're often baseless.

What Are Mind Reading and Fortune-Telling?

These distortions involve jumping to conclusions without evidence:

1.Mind Reading:

Believing you know what others are thinking—usually something negative about you.

Example: "They didn't respond to my email because they're upset with me."

2.Fortune-Telling:

Predicting the future, assuming the worst will happen.

Example: "I'm going to fail this interview. There's no way I'll get the job."

While they feel intuitive, these thought patterns are often driven by fear, self-doubt, or past experiences rather than reality.

How These Distortions Impact Life

Mind reading and fortune-telling can significantly affect your confidence, relationships, and decision-making:

1.Eroding Confidence:

Assuming others are judging you can lead to feelings of inadequacy or imposter syndrome.

2.Strained Relationships:

Misinterpreting others' intentions can cause unnecessary conflict or withdrawal.

3.Avoidance and Procrastination:

Predicting failure may stop you from pursuing opportunities or taking risks.

4.Chronic Anxiety:

Constantly expecting the worst can create a state of heightened stress and fear.

Why Do We Engage in Mind Reading and Fortune-Telling?

These distortions stem from our brain's tendency to make quick judgments, often based on incomplete information. This habit is rooted in:

Past Experiences:

Negative encounters can create assumptions that similar situations will turn out the same way.

Fear of Rejection:

Mind reading and fortune-telling often reflect a deep-seated fear of failure, criticism, or rejection.

Need for Certainty:

Predicting the future—however inaccurately—can feel like a way to prepare for the unknown.

Unfortunately, these shortcuts rarely lead to accurate conclusions and often amplify feelings of stress and insecurity.

Breaking Free from Mind Reading and Fortune-Telling

The key to overcoming these distortions is learning to challenge your assumptions and focus on evidence rather than fear.

1. Look for Evidence:

Ask yourself:

"What evidence do I have that this thought is true?"

"What evidence contradicts it?"

For example:

Thought: "They didn't say hi to me—they must be upset."

Evidence: "They've been friendly in the past. Maybe they were distracted or having a bad day."

2. Reframe the Thought:

Replace assumptions with curiosity. Instead of "They think I'm incompetent," try:

"I don't know what they're thinking. I can ask for feedback if I'm unsure."

For fortune-telling:

Replace "I'll fail this project" with "I don't know how it will go, but I'll prepare my best."

3. Check for Cognitive Biases:

Mind reading and fortune-telling often involve mental shortcuts, like focusing on negative possibilities or overgeneralizing. Challenge these biases:

"*Am I assuming the worst without considering other possibilities?*"

"*Could this thought be influenced by my own insecurities?*"

4. Ask for Clarification:

If you're uncertain about someone's thoughts or intentions, don't guess—ask.

Example: "I noticed you seemed quiet earlier. Is everything okay?"

5. Focus on the Present Moment:

Mind reading and fortune-telling pull you into imaginary scenarios. Ground yourself in the present by asking:

"*What is happening right now, and how can I respond?*"

Case Study: Challenging Assumptions

The Situation:
Liam, a 29-year-old software developer, presents an idea during a team meeting. Afterward, one colleague doesn't make eye contact or comment on the proposal. Liam thinks:

"They must think my idea was stupid."

The Challenge:
Liam pauses and examines the evidence:

Has this colleague given feedback before? Yes, usually positive.

Could there be other reasons for their behavior? Yes—they might be distracted or preoccupied.

The Reframe:
Liam reminds himself: "I don't know what they're thinking. Instead of assuming the worst, I can ask for their feedback later."

When he follows up, the colleague praises his idea and apologizes for being distracted by a personal matter during the meeting.

Moving Forward

Mind reading and fortune-telling are like mental traps, pulling you into imagined worlds of judgment and failure. By questioning your assumptions and focusing on evidence, you can free yourself from these distortions and approach situations with clarity and confidence.

*In the next chapter, we'll explore **Labeling and Mislabeling**, the distortions that reduce complex experiences into harsh, simplistic judgments. If you've ever thought, "I'm such a failure," this chapter will help you see yourself in a new light.*

9.Labeling and Mislabeling

"I Am My Mistakes."

The Danger of Defining Yourself by a Single Event

Picture this: You spill coffee on your shirt during a meeting, and the thought strikes you like lightning:

"I'm so clumsy."

Or maybe you miss a deadline at work and your mind spirals:

"I'm such a failure. I can't do anything right."

*This is **labeling**, a cognitive distortion where you define yourself—or others—by a single action, mistake, or perceived flaw. It's a way of oversimplifying complex human behavior into one harsh, unchanging identity.*

What Is Labeling and Mislabeling?

Labeling involves attaching a sweeping, negative label to yourself or someone else based on a specific behavior or incident. Mislabeling takes this a step further, using exaggerated or emotionally charged language to reinforce the label.

Labeling Yourself:

Example: "I failed the test. I'm a loser."

Labeling Others:

Example: "He cut me off in traffic. What a jerk!"

Mislabeling:

Example: "I messed up at work today. I'm completely useless and pathetic."

Labeling overshadows nuance and complexity, creating an identity that feels permanent and inescapable.

Why We Label Ourselves and Others

Labeling often stems from the brain's natural tendency to simplify information. Processing the world in absolutes—good or bad, success or failure—feels easier than navigating shades of gray.

However, this oversimplification can lead to distorted thinking, particularly when:

Emotions Run High:

Stress, frustration, or embarrassment can push you to make quick, extreme judgments.

Past Beliefs Take Over:

Childhood labels (e.g., "the troublemaker" or "the shy one") can stick with you, influencing how you see yourself.

Fear of Vulnerability:

Labeling others harshly can act as a defense mechanism, keeping you from empathizing or addressing complex feelings.

The Cost of Labeling and Mislabeling

Labels are limiting. When you define yourself—or others—by a single moment or characteristic, you:

1.Undermine Growth:

Seeing yourself as "stupid" or "incompetent" can stop you from trying new things or improving.

2.Damage Relationships:

Labeling others as "selfish" or "lazy" can prevent meaningful communication or understanding.

3.Reinforce Negative Beliefs:

Negative labels create a feedback loop, where you focus on behaviors that confirm the label while ignoring evidence to the contrary.

4.Erode Self-Esteem:

Reducing yourself to your mistakes makes it difficult to see your strengths and potential.

Breaking Free from Labels

Overcoming labeling involves challenging rigid definitions and embracing the complexity of human behavior. Here's how:

1. Challenge the Label:
Ask yourself:

"Is this label accurate, or am I oversimplifying?"

"Does one action define me—or anyone else?"

For example:

Label: "I'm such a failure."

Reframe: "I made a mistake, but that doesn't define my entire worth."

2. Focus on Specific Behaviors:
Separate the action from the person.

Instead of: "I'm a bad parent."

Say: "I lost my temper with my child today. I can work on being more patient."

This shift helps you address the behavior without internalizing it as a permanent identity.

3. Recognize Nuance and Complexity:
Remind yourself that people, including you, are a mix of strengths and weaknesses. No one is perfect, and no single action defines a person.

Example: "I missed a deadline at work, but I've met many others. This mistake doesn't define me."

4. Replace Negative Labels with Neutral Descriptions:
Practice describing yourself and others in less judgmental terms.

Instead of: "I'm lazy."

Say: "I've been feeling unmotivated lately. I can figure out why and take steps to change it."

5. Practice Self-Compassion:

Treat yourself with the same kindness you would offer a friend. Remind yourself that mistakes are a natural part of growth.

Example: "It's okay to have an off day. This doesn't mean I'm a failure."

Case Study: Moving Beyond Labels

The Situation:

Sophia, a 40-year-old entrepreneur, makes a miscalculation that causes her company to lose a key client. She thinks:

"I'm such a terrible business owner. I don't deserve to lead this company."

The Challenge:

Sophia works with a mentor to separate her actions from her identity:

"Have I made successful decisions in the past?" Yes.

"Does one mistake erase all the good I've done?" No.

The Reframe:
Sophia replaces her label with a balanced perspective:

"I made a mistake that hurt the business, but I've learned from it and can rebuild trust with my clients."

This shift allows Sophia to move forward with confidence and resilience.

Moving Forward

Labels are shortcuts that simplify complex realities, but they rarely tell the full story. By challenging labels and embracing nuance, you can see yourself—and others—with greater compassion and clarity.

*In the next chapter, we'll explore **Overcoming Cognitive Distortions as a Whole**, integrating the lessons we've learned into a holistic approach for building healthier, more balanced thinking.*

• • •

CHAPTER IV

"Rewiring Your Mind: A Comprehensive Guide to Conquering Cognitive Distortions"

"Neurons that fire together wire together." – Donald Hebb

The Path to Mental Clarity

Throughout this journey, we've explored the most common cognitive distortions—those invisible traps that shape our thoughts, emotions, and behaviors. Whether it's catastrophizing about the future, personalizing others' emotions, or labeling ourselves unfairly, these patterns can feel overwhelming and automatic.

But here's the truth: **Cognitive distortions are habits, not facts.**

And like any habit, they can be unlearned with awareness, effort, and practice. This chapter is about weaving together the tools and strategies we've discussed into a comprehensive approach that helps you rewrite your mental patterns and cultivate resilience, clarity, and emotional balance.

The Framework for Change

Rewiring your thinking is a process that requires patience and persistence. Here's a step-by-step framework to guide you:

1. Build Awareness: Spot the Distortions

You can't change what you don't recognize. Start by paying attention to your thought patterns:

Keep a Thought Journal:
Write down moments when you feel upset, anxious, or frustrated. Note the thoughts running through your mind and see if you can identify any cognitive distortions.

Use a Checklist of Distortions:
Refer to the distortions we've explored—such as catastrophizing, all-or-nothing thinking, or mental filtering—and see which ones resonate with your thoughts.

2. Pause and Question: Challenge the Thought

Once you've identified a distortion, step back and challenge it:

Ask for Evidence:

"What facts support this thought?"

"What evidence contradicts it?"

Explore Alternative Explanations:

"Could there be another reason for this situation?"

"Am I overlooking something positive or neutral?"

Imagine You're Advising a Friend:

What would you say to someone else who had this thought? Often, we're kinder and more rational with others than we are with ourselves.

3. Reframe and Rewrite: Replace the Thought

Shift your perspective by replacing distorted thoughts with balanced, constructive ones.

Example:

Distorted Thought: "I failed this project. I'm a failure."

Reframe: "This project didn't go as planned, but I've succeeded in other areas. I can learn from this and improve."

4. Practice Mindfulness: Stay Grounded in the Present

Cognitive distortions often pull you into the past (regret, guilt) or the future (fear, worry). Mindfulness helps you return to the present moment.

Mindful Breathing:

Focus on your breath to calm your mind and create space between you and your thoughts.

Observe Without Judgment:

Notice your thoughts as they arise, without labeling them as "good" or "bad." This detachment makes it easier to let go of distorted thinking.

5. Create New Mental Habits

Overcoming cognitive distortions isn't just about challenging negative thoughts—it's about building new, healthier habits of thinking.

Focus on Positivity:
Train your brain to notice the good by keeping a gratitude journal or reflecting on daily successes.

Set Realistic Standards:
Replace perfectionism with progress. Aim for "good enough" instead of "perfect."

Celebrate Growth:
Acknowledge small victories in rewiring your thinking. Each step forward is progress.

6. Seek Support When Needed

Rewiring your thinking doesn't have to be a solo journey. If you're struggling to overcome deeply ingrained distortions, consider seeking help:

Therapy: *Cognitive Behavioral Therapy (CBT) is particularly effective for identifying and challenging cognitive distortions.*

Support Groups: *Sharing experiences with others can provide new perspectives and reduce feelings of isolation.*

Trusted Friends or Mentors: *A supportive person can help you reality-check your thoughts and offer encouragement.*

Bringing It All Together: A Holistic Example

Case 1: Overgeneralization in a Young Professional

Situation:
Meera, a 27-year-old software engineer from Bengaluru, failed to meet a tight deadline for a project. She thought, "I always fail at everything. I'll never succeed in this job."

Distortion:
Overgeneralization – Taking one incident and assuming it represents a pattern of failure in all areas of life.

Rewiring Process:

1.Identifying the Thought: *Meera began tracking her negative thoughts using a thought journal.*

2.Challenging the Thought: *She asked herself, "Is it true that I fail at everything? What about the successful projects I've completed in the past?"*

3.Reframing the Thought: *Meera replaced her original thought with, "I missed one deadline due to unforeseen circumstances, but I've succeeded in other areas. This is a learning experience, not a defining moment."*

Outcome:
By practicing this reframing process, Meera regained her confidence and successfully led the next project to completion.

Case 2: Catastrophizing in a College Student

Situation:
Rajesh, a 21-year-old college student in Delhi, failed his first attempt at a public speaking competition. He thought, "I embarrassed myself in front of everyone. I'll never be good at public speaking, and my classmates will always judge me."

Distortion:
Catastrophizing – Blowing a single event out of proportion and imagining the worst possible outcomes.

Rewiring Process:

1.Grounding with Evidence: Rajesh's mentor encouraged him to list evidence against his fear of judgment. He realized that most classmates appreciated his effort and encouraged him to try again.

2.Creating a Plan: Instead of giving up, Rajesh attended a public speaking workshop to build his skills.

3.Reframing the Situation: He replaced his catastrophic thought with, "This was one attempt, and it didn't go perfectly. With practice, I can improve and perform better next time."

Outcome:
Rajesh competed again and won second place in his next competition, proving to himself that failure isn't permanent.

Case 3: Personalization in a Homemaker

Situation:
Anita, a 35-year-old homemaker from Jaipur, felt responsible for her teenage son's poor grades. She thought, "If I were a better parent, he wouldn't struggle in school. I'm failing him."

Distortion:
Personalization – Taking excessive responsibility for outcomes beyond one's control.

Rewiring Process:

1.Separating Responsibility: *Anita worked with a counselor to understand that her son's academic struggles were influenced by multiple factors, not solely her parenting.*

2.Balanced Thinking: *She reframed her thought to, "I support my son as much as I can, but his performance is also influenced by his efforts and other circumstances."*

3.Collaborative Action: *Anita collaborated with her son's teachers to create a supportive study plan and encouraged him to take ownership of his learning.*

Outcome:
Anita reduced her guilt and improved her relationship with her son by focusing on constructive support rather than self-blame.

Case 4: Should Statements in a Teacher

Situation:
Vikram, a 45-year-old school teacher from Pune, often told himself, "I should be able to manage my workload without getting tired. I must always meet every student's needs perfectly."

Distortion:
Should Statements – Rigid expectations that create guilt or frustration when not met.

Rewiring Process:

1.Challenging the Shoulds: *Vikram identified the pressure he placed on himself and asked, "Is it realistic to expect perfection from myself all the time?"*

2.Replacing Shoulds with Balanced Statements: *He replaced "I must always be perfect" with "I strive to do my best, but it's okay to take breaks and set boundaries."*

3.Self-Compassion: *Vikram began practicing self-compassion, reminding himself that imperfection is part of being human.*

Outcome:
By letting go of unrealistic expectations, Vikram experienced reduced stress and was able to approach his teaching with renewed energy and balance.

Case 5: Mind Reading in a Young Entrepreneur

Situation:
Pooja, a 30-year-old entrepreneur from Mumbai, felt anxious after pitching her business idea to potential investors. She thought, "They were so quiet during my presentation. They must think my idea is terrible."

Distortion:
Mind Reading – Assuming you know what others are thinking without evidence.

Rewiring Process:

1.Reality Check: *Pooja reminded herself that silence doesn't necessarily indicate judgment and could mean the investors were processing her pitch.*

2.Seeking Feedback: *Instead of assuming, Pooja reached out to the investors for feedback. She learned they were impressed but wanted more details about her marketing plan.*

3.Reframing the Thought: *Pooja replaced her thought with, "Their silence doesn't mean rejection. I'll clarify their doubts to strengthen my proposal."*

Outcome:
Pooja gained valuable insights from the investors and secured funding in her second meeting.

Case 6: Labeling, Mind Reading, and Catastrophizing in a Teacher

Situation:
Aarti, a 28-year-old teacher from Chennai, receives feedback from her supervisor suggesting that her lesson plan could use more creativity. She immediately

assumes, *"I'm such a bad teacher. My students must hate my lessons. What if I lose my job?"*

Distortions:

1.Labeling: *Defining herself as a "bad teacher" based on one piece of feedback.*

2.Mind Reading: *Assuming her students hate her lessons without any evidence.*

3.Catastrophizing: *Imagining the worst-case scenario of losing her job.*

Rewiring Process:

1.

Build Awareness:
Aarti begins tracking her thoughts in a journal and identifies the distortions affecting her perception. She notices the pattern of labeling, mind reading, and catastrophizing in her response to feedback.

2.

Pause and Question:

3.

Evidence Check: *Aarti asks herself, "What proof do I have that I'm a bad teacher?" She recalls* *positive feedback from her students in the past, which contradicts her negative belief.*

4.

Alternative Explanation: *She considers that her supervisor might simply want to encourage her growth and help her improve, rather than criticize her overall ability.*

5.

Reframe and Rewrite:
Aarti replaces her original thoughts with a balanced perspective:

"This feedback is constructive, not a judgment of my teaching skills. I can use it as an opportunity to improve and enhance my lessons."

Practice Mindfulness:
To reduce her anxiety, Aarti takes deep breaths and focuses on the present moment. She reminds herself, "My thoughts are not facts; they're just temporary reactions."

Create New Habits:

Aarti decides to incorporate one creative idea into her next lesson to act on the feedback.

She starts a journal to document her teaching successes, helping her build confidence by focusing on her strengths and achievements.

Outcome:

By reframing her thoughts and taking proactive steps, Aarti not only improves her lesson plans but also strengthens her self-confidence. She learns to view feedback as an opportunity for growth rather than a measure of her worth.

These real-life examples demonstrate that rewiring your thinking is not only possible but also transformative. By identifying cognitive distortions, challenging their validity, and replacing them with constructive thoughts, individuals from all walks of life can overcome self-imposed limitations and unlock their potential.

Your Ongoing Journey

Rewiring your thinking isn't about eliminating every distorted thought—it's about creating a mental environment where those thoughts no longer control you. Over time, the tools you've learned will become second nature, helping you navigate challenges with clarity and confidence.

The Power of Resilience

By recognizing and challenging cognitive distortions, you're not just changing your thoughts—you're transforming your life. Each small shift in perspective builds resilience, allowing you to face difficulties with strength and grace.

This journey is ongoing, but every step forward matters. Be patient with yourself, celebrate your progress, and remember: **you are not your thoughts.**

Closing Words

The human mind is powerful, capable of both constructing and dismantling the barriers that hold us back. By understanding cognitive distortions and learning to reframe them, you've taken a vital step toward greater clarity, emotional freedom, and self-compassion.

As you move forward, keep this mantra in mind:

I am more than my thoughts. I am capable of growth, resilience, and change.

The tools are now in your hands. Use them to build a brighter, more balanced perspective—and a life that feels aligned with your true potential.

CHAPTER V

Workbook Template

1.Cognitive Distortions Checklist

1.

All-or-Nothing Thinking: Viewing situations in black-and-white terms, with no room for nuance."If I'm not perfect, I'm a failure."

2.

Overgeneralization: Drawing broad conclusions from a single event or limited evidence."I failed this test, so I'll fail every test."

3.

Mental Filtering: Focusing only on the negatives while ignoring the positives."I got good feedback, but I'm fixated on the one criticism."

4.

Catastrophizing: Imagining the worst-case scenario or exaggerating a problem."If I miss this deadline, my career is over."

5.

Personalization: Taking responsibility for things outside your control."They're upset because I didn't do enough."

6.

Emotional Reasoning: Believing that your feelings reflect reality."I feel scared, so something bad must be happening."

7.

Should Statements: Imposing rigid rules or expectations on yourself or others."I should never make mistakes, or I'm a failure."

8.

Mind Reading: Assuming you know what others are thinking without evidence."They didn't say hi, so they must dislike me."

9.

Fortune-Telling: Predicting a negative future without evidence."I just know I'll fail the interview."

10.

Labeling: Reducing yourself or others to a single negative label."I made a mistake; I'm an idiot."

11.

Mislabeling: Using exaggerated, emotionally charged labels."I'm a total disaster because I messed up."

12.

Discounting the Positive: Rejecting positive experiences or accomplishments as insignificant."They said I did well, but they were just being nice."

13.

Comparisons: Comparing yourself negatively to others while ignoring your strengths.“They're so much more successful than me.”

Instructions

1.

   Identify the Thought: *Write down a thought or situation you're struggling with.*

2.

   Review the Checklist: *Match the thought with distortions in the table above.*

3.

   Challenge and Reframe: *Use tools like evidence-checking, alternative explanations, or positive reframing to address the distortion.*

This table provides a practical way to track, understand, and correct cognitive distortions as they arise.

<u>2.Thought Workbook Tool</u>

The **Thought Workbook Tool** is a structured guide to help individuals identify, analyze, and reframe cognitive distortions. By working through this tool regularly, you can develop greater awareness of your thought patterns and learn to replace unhelpful thoughts with balanced, constructive ones.

Step

Your Response

1. Situation:-

2. Automatic Thoughts:-

3. Emotions:-

4. Cognitive Distortions:-

5. Challenging Questions:-

6. Reframed Thoughts:-

7. New Perspective:-

Tips for Using the Workbook

1.

   Consistency: *Use the workbook daily or whenever a challenging situation arises.*

2.

   Honesty: *Be truthful about your thoughts and emotions, even if they feel uncomfortable.*

3.

   Patience: *Rewiring your thinking takes time—practice these steps regularly to see long-term benefits.*

4.

   Support: *Share your workbook with a therapist or mentor for additional guidance and feedback.*

The Thought Workbook Tool is a powerful resource for breaking free from cognitive distortions and cultivating a healthier, more balanced mindset.

<u>3. Emotional Awareness Journal</u>

Purpose: *Helps individuals identify and understand their emotions, linking them to specific triggers and thoughts.*

How to Use:

- *Record daily emotional experiences.*

- *Note the intensity of each emotion (scale of 1–10).*

- *Identify the event or thought that triggered the emotion.*

- *Reflect on whether the emotion aligns with reality or is distorted by cognitive patterns.*

4. Gratitude Practice Tool

Purpose:
Helps you focus on the positive aspects of life, shifting attention away from negativity and fostering a sense of appreciation.

How to Use:

Write down three specific things you're grateful for each day.

Include why they matter to you to deepen your reflection.

Examples:

1. I'm grateful for the warm cup of tea I had this morning. It gave me a moment of calm before a busy day.

2. I'm grateful for my friend's call today. It reminded me I'm not alone and that I'm supported.

3. I'm grateful for the cool breeze during my evening walk. It helped me relax and clear my mind.

This simple practice shifts your focus to the positives and builds emotional resilience over time.

5. Mindfulness and Grounding Exercises

Purpose: *Brings attention to the present moment to reduce anxiety and overthinking.*

How to Use:

- **Breathing Exercises:** *Focus on slow, deep breaths for 5 minutes. Inhale for 4 seconds, hold for 4 seconds, and exhale for 6 seconds.*

5-4-3-2-1 Technique: *Identify 5 things you see, 4 you can touch, 3 you hear, 2 you smell, and 1 you taste.*

6. Affirmation Builder

Purpose: *Replaces self-critical thoughts with empowering beliefs.*

How to Use: *1.Identify a negative thought or belief.*

2.Write a positive affirmation to counter it.

3.Repeat the affirmation daily morning and evening or during challenging situations.

Rules for Creating Effective Affirmations

1.

Positive Language: *Focus on what you want, not what you want to avoid. E.g., "I am calm" instead of "I don't want to be anxious."*

2.

Specific and Clear: *Define your goal clearly. E.g., "I complete tasks efficiently."*

3.

Present Tense: *Write as if it's already true. E.g., "I am confident," not "I will be confident."*

4.

Believable: *Ensure it feels realistic. E.g., "I am improving daily," not "I am perfect."*

5.

Action-Oriented: *Highlight growth and effort. E.g., "I am learning every day."*

6.

Personalized: *Use "I" to make it about you. E.g., "I trust myself to succeed."*

7.

Short and Memorable: *Keep it concise. E.g., "I am worthy of success."*

8.

Emotion-Focused:*Add positive feelings. E.g.,"I feel grateful for my progress."*

9.

Repeat Daily: *Reinforce belief with consistency.*

10.

Pair with Action: *Align affirmations with efforts. E.g., Affirm: "I am organized," Action: Plan your day.*

Short, clear, and actionable affirmations can transform your mindset effectively!

7. Action-Oriented Problem-Solving Tool

Purpose:
Encourages practical and proactive steps to address worries and challenges, turning obstacles into manageable tasks.

How to Use:

Write Down the Problem: Clearly identify the issue you're facing.

Example: "I'm overwhelmed with preparing for my final exams."

Brainstorm Actionable Solutions: List specific, realistic steps you could take to address the problem.

Example:

Break study material into smaller sections.

Set up a daily study schedule.

Ask a teacher or friend for help with tough topics.

Identify the First Small Step: *Choose one simple action to get started.*

Example: *"Review the syllabus and make a study timetable for the week."*

Reflect and Adjust: *After taking action, evaluate how it went. If needed, tweak your plan to improve outcomes.*

Example: *"The timetable helped me stay on track, but I'll add short breaks to stay fresh."*

By breaking problems into actionable steps, this tool helps you focus on progress rather than feeling stuck.

8. Thought-to-Action Tracker

Purpose: *Connects your thoughts to actions and outcomes, helping you identify patterns and make intentional changes for better results.*

How to Use: *Write Down a Thought or Belief: Capture the thought that influenced your behavior.*

Example: *"I'll fail this exam because I'm not smart enough."*

Note the Action You Took Because of That Thought: *Record what you did as a result of that belief.*

Example: *"Avoided studying altogether because I felt it wouldn't help."*

Reflect on the Outcome and Whether It Matched Your Expectations: *Analyze what happened and how it compared to what you expected.*

Example: *"I felt even more stressed and unprepared, which confirmed my initial fear of failure."*

Plan an Alternative Action for Similar Future Thoughts: *Decide on a healthier action to take if the same thought arises.*

Example: "Instead of avoiding studying, I'll break the material into smaller sections and focus on one topic at a time."

Additional Example:

Thought: *"They didn't reply to my message—they must dislike me."*

Action: *Avoided reaching out again and distanced myself.*

Outcome: *The misunderstanding grew, and I felt lonelier.*

Alternative Action: *"Next time, I'll ask them directly if everything is okay to clear up any confusion."*

This tracker helps you identify how thoughts influence actions and equips you with strategies to respond differently for better outcomes.

9. Self-Compassion Toolkit

Purpose:
Fosters a kinder, more supportive relationship with yourself, helping you navigate challenges with empathy and self-acceptance.

How to Use:

Reflect on What You'd Say to a Friend in the Same Situation:
Imagine a friend experiencing the same struggle. Consider the kind, understanding words you'd offer them.

Example: "If my friend failed an exam, I'd tell them, 'One setback doesn't define your abilities. You've done well before, and you'll succeed again with some effort.'"

Write a Supportive Letter or Thought for Yourself:
Put into words the encouragement you need to hear. Write it as though you're speaking to someone you care about deeply.

Example:
Dear Me,
It's okay to feel disappointed right now, but remember

that one exam doesn't determine your worth. You've faced tough situations before and found ways to overcome them. This is just a step in your journey—not the end. Keep going; you're capable of amazing things.

Highlight Your Strengths and Resilience:
Take a moment to list qualities and past successes that demonstrate your ability to persevere.

Example:

I'm hardworking and always try my best.

I've overcome challenges like learning new skills during my internship.

I care deeply about my goals, which motivates me to keep improving.

Additional Example:

Situation: *Made a mistake at work.*

What You'd Say to a Friend: *"Everyone makes mistakes—it's how we learn. You're still good at your job, and this is just a bump in the road."*

Supportive Thought: *"I'm learning from this mistake, and it doesn't define my capabilities. I've succeeded in many other tasks before."*

Strengths and Resilience: *"I've shown resourcefulness under pressure, and I'm committed to doing better."*

This toolkit nurtures self-compassion by shifting your inner dialogue from criticism to care, building resilience and emotional well-being.

10. Weekly Reflection and Goal-Setting Tool

Purpose:
This tool helps you evaluate your week's accomplishments and obstacles, identify thinking patterns, and set actionable goals for improvement. It fosters self-awareness and growth.

How to Use:

Reflect on the Successes and Challenges of Your Week:
Write down moments where you excelled and areas that were difficult.

Example:

Successes: "I completed my assignments on time and helped a friend with their project."

Challenges: "I procrastinated on studying for a test and felt overwhelmed."

Identify Any Cognitive Distortions Influencing Your Thought Patterns or Decisions:
Recognize if distorted thinking impacted your week.

Example:

Distortion Identified: *Catastrophizing.*

Thought: *"If I don't do well on this test, I'll fail the entire course."*

Impact: *Avoided studying, which increased stress.*

Set a Specific, Actionable Goal to Address Challenges or Improve Habits:
Plan one concrete step to work on in the coming week.

Example:

Goal: *Break study material into smaller chunks and dedicate 1 hour daily to revision.*

Ready-to-Use Example:

Week of: YYYY-MM-DD

Reflection:

Successes:

Completed all work meetings on time.

Exercised three days this week.

Challenges:

Felt anxious during a team presentation.

Avoided discussing feedback with my manager.

| Cognitive Distortion Noticed:

Mind Reading: "They must think I'm not good at my job."

Impact: I avoided a valuable conversation that could have helped me grow.

| Goal for Next Week:

Action Step: Schedule a meeting with my manager to discuss feedback and prepare questions in advance to reduce anxiety.

This tool allows you to track growth over time, fostering a sense of progress and mindfulness in daily actions.

11. Visualization Exercise for Balanced Thinking

Purpose: This exercise helps you replace distorted thoughts with balanced and realistic perspectives by imagining positive scenarios. It builds calmness, confidence, and a sense of control in stressful situations.

How to Use: Identify a Specific Situation Where You Anticipate Distorted Thinking:
Choose a challenging scenario that tends to trigger negative thoughts. For example, giving a presentation at school or work.

Note the Distorted Thought and Write a More Balanced Alternative:
Reflect on the automatic negative thought and reframe it into a constructive perspective.

Distorted Thought: "I'll mess up, and everyone will laugh at me."

Balanced Alternative: "I've prepared thoroughly, and it's okay to make small mistakes. Most people will appreciate my effort."

Visualize the Balanced Scenario and Reflect on How It Made You Feel:

Close your eyes and vividly imagine yourself handling the situation successfully. Picture the details: your calm body language, your confident tone, and positive reactions from others. Afterward, reflect on how this visualization affects your emotions.

Example Reflection: *"Seeing myself succeed in my mind helped me feel less anxious and more capable of handling the situation in real life."*

Example Application: *For a student nervous about presenting in front of a class:*

They imagine standing confidently, speaking clearly, and noticing classmates nodding in agreement.

Instead of focusing on their fear of failure, they focus on the effort and preparation they've put in.

After visualizing, they feel a renewed sense of calm and optimism, realizing that their fears were exaggerated.

By practicing this regularly, you can train your mind to respond more positively and realistically to stress-inducing situations.

• • •

155

CHAPTER VI

Myths and Facts About Thinking Errors

Introduction:
Thinking errors, or cognitive distortions, are universal experiences, yet they are often misunderstood. This chapter separates myths from facts to provide a clearer understanding and dispel misconceptions that may hinder growth.

Myth 1: Thinking Errors Only Happen to People with Mental Health Problems

Fact: *Thinking errors are common to all humans. They arise because the brain takes shortcuts to process vast amounts of information. While they are more pronounced in conditions like anxiety or depression, everyone experiences them at some point.*

Myth 2: Thinking Errors Are Just Bad Habits That Can't Be Changed

Fact: *While thinking errors are habitual, they are not permanent. With awareness and practice, you can rewire your mind and develop healthier thought patterns, thanks to neuroplasticity—the brain's ability to adapt and change.*

Myth 3: Positive Thinking Alone Can Eliminate Thinking Errors

Fact: Positive thinking can be helpful, but it's not a cure-all. Overcoming thinking errors involves identifying distortions, challenging them, and replacing them with balanced thoughts—not simply covering them up with positivity.

Myth 4: Thinking Errors Are Always Harmful

Fact: Not all thinking errors are harmful. For example, a mild form of catastrophizing may help you prepare for challenges. However, when left unchecked, these patterns can escalate and negatively impact emotions and decisions.

Myth 5: Thinking Errors Are a Sign of Weakness

Fact: Experiencing thinking errors doesn't reflect weakness; it reflects human nature. Our brains are wired to use cognitive shortcuts to save energy and time, but these shortcuts can sometimes lead to errors. Recognizing and addressing them is a sign of strength, not weakness.

Myth 6: If I Change My Thoughts, My Emotions Will Instantly Improve

Fact: Changing thoughts is a process that takes time and effort. While reframing your thinking can lead to better emotional balance, it often requires consistent practice to create lasting change.

Myth 7: Thinking Errors Only Affect the Way We Feel

Fact: Thinking errors influence not only emotions but also behaviors, decisions, relationships, and even physical health. By addressing distorted thinking, you improve multiple aspects of your life.

Myth 8: You Have to Eliminate All Thinking Errors

Fact: It's impossible to completely eliminate thinking errors because they are a natural part of how the brain processes information. The goal is not to eradicate them but to recognize when they occur and respond to them effectively.

Conclusion:

Understanding the myths and facts about thinking errors helps you approach them with compassion and clarity. Instead of seeing them as fixed flaws, view them as opportunities for growth. By breaking down these misconceptions, you empower yourself to engage with your thoughts more mindfully and begin the journey toward greater mental clarity and peace.

References:

1. Arnsten, A. F. T. et al. (2013). The neurobiology of stress: implications for cognition and behavior. *Nature Reviews Neuroscience*, 14(6), 409–418.
2. Etkin, A., & Wager, T. D. (2007). Functional neuroimaging of anxiety: A meta-analysis. *American Journal of Psychiatry*, 164(10), 1476–1488.
3. Bremner, J. D. et al. (2004). Neuroanatomical correlates of trauma exposure and post-traumatic stress disorder. *Annals of the New York Academy of Sciences*, 1032(1), 1–9.
4. Harmer, C. J. et al. (2007). Serotonin and emotional processing: Does it help explain antidepressant drug action? *Neuropsychopharmacology*, 33(5), 1148–1158.
5. Lupien, S. J. et al. (2009). Effects of stress throughout the lifespan on the brain, behavior, and cognition. *Nature Reviews Neuroscience*, 10(6), 434–445.
6. Pizzagalli, D. A. (2014). Depression, stress, and anhedonia: Toward a synthesis and integrated model. *Annual Review of Clinical Psychology*, 10, 393–423.
7. Siegle, G. J., Thompson, W., Carter, C. S., Steinhauer, S. R., & Thase, M. E. (2007). Increased activity in the prefrontal cortex following cognitive therapy for depression: Evidence from neuroimaging. *Neuropsychopharmacology*, 32(8), 1620-1629.
8. Goldin, P. R., Ziv, M., Jazaieri, H., Werner, K., Kraemer, H., Heimberg, R. G., & Gross, J. J. (2016). Cognitive reappraisal self-efficacy mediates the effects of individual cognitive-behavioral therapy for social anxiety disorder. *Journal of Anxiety Disorders*, 37, 43-54.
9. Davidson, R. J., & McEwen, B. S. (2013). Social influences on neuroplasticity: Stress and interventions to promote well-being.

Nature Neuroscience, 15(5), 689-695.

10. Hölzel, B. K., Carmody, J., Vangel, M., Congleton, C., Yerramsetti, S. M., Gard, T., & Lazar, S. W. (2016). Mindfulness practice leads to increases in regional brain gray matter density. *Psychiatry Research: Neuroimaging, 191*(1), 36-43.

11. Yehuda, R., et al. (2005). Transgenerational effects of posttraumatic stress disorder in offspring of Holocaust survivors. *Biological Psychiatry, 57*(5), 430-433.

12. McGowan, P. O., et al. (2009). Epigenetic regulation of the glucocorticoid receptor in human brain associates with childhood abuse. *Nature Neuroscience, 12*(3), 342-348.

13. Kaliman, P., et al. (2014). Rapid changes in histone deacetylases and inflammatory gene expression in expert meditators. *Psychoneuroendocrinology, 40*, 96-107.

14. Beck, A. T. (1979). *Cognitive Therapy of Depression.* New York: Guilford Press.

15. Burns, D. D. (1980). *Feeling Good: The New Mood Therapy.* New York: HarperCollins.

16. Seligman, M. E. P. (2002). *Authentic Happiness: Using the New Positive Psychology to Realize Your Potential for Lasting Fulfillment.* New York: Free Press.

17. Neff, K. (2011). *Self-Compassion: The Proven Power of Being Kind to Yourself.* New York: HarperCollins.

18. Kabat-Zinn, J. (1990). *Full Catastrophe Living: Using the Wisdom of Your Body and Mind to Face Stress, Pain, and Illness.* New York: Bantam Books.

19. Aronson, E., Wilson, T. D., & Akert, R. M. (2018). *Social Psychology.* Boston: Pearson.

20. Hofmann, S. G., Asnaani, A., Vonk, I. J., Sawyer, A. T., & Fang, A. (2012). The efficacy of cognitive behavioral therapy: A review of meta-analyses. *Cognitive Therapy and Research, 36*(5), 427-440.

21. Mikulincer, M., & Shaver, P. R. (2017). Attachment in adulthood: Structure, dynamics, and change (2nd ed.). New York: Guilford Press.

REFERENCES:

22. Fraley, R. C., & Shaver, P. R. (2000). Adult romantic attachment: Theoretical developments, emerging controversies, and unanswered questions. *Review of General Psychology,* 4(2), 132-154.
23. Siegel, D. J. (2012). *The Developing Mind: How Relationships and the Brain Interact to Shape Who We Are.* New York: Guilford Press.
24. Taylor, S. E. (2006). Tend and befriend: Biobehavioral bases of affiliation under stress. *Current Directions in Psychological Science,* 15(6), 273-277.
25. Carver, C. S., & Scheier, M. F. (1998). *On the Self-Regulation of Behavior.* New York: Cambridge University Press.
26. Lazarus, R. S., & Folkman, S. (1984). *Stress, Appraisal, and Coping.* New York: Springer.
27. Linehan, M. M. (1993). *Cognitive-Behavioral Treatment of Borderline Personality Disorder.* New York: Guilford Press.
28. Shapiro, S. L., Carlson, L. E., Astin, J. A., & Freedman, B. (2006). Mechanisms of mindfulness. *Journal of Clinical Psychology,* 62(3), 373-386.
29. Vivek G Vasoya MD, "Mind Over Matter: A Guide to Cognitive Behavioral Therapy", "Mind Over Matter: A Guide to Cognitive Behavioral Therapy" eBook ; Vasoya MD Psychiatrist, Dr.Vivek G ; Amazon.in: Kindle Store
30. Vivek G Vasoya MD, Unleashing Your Potential: A Journey of Self-Discovery and Personal Growth, https://www.amazon.in/Unleashing-Your-Potential-Self-Discovery-Personal-ebook/dp/B0C6PQBW2X

www.ingramcontent.com/pod-product-compliance
Lightning Source LLC
Chambersburg PA
CBHW031133130726
47988CB00006B/2355